What's This?

The Cicada   2

The Sea Urchin   4

The Monarch Butterfly   6

The Dandelion   8

The Thrush   10

The Nurseryweb Spider   12

The Pine Tree   14

What Can You Find Out About These?   16

A READ-ABOUT

The Cicada

This is the skin of a cicada. It was found on a tree trunk.

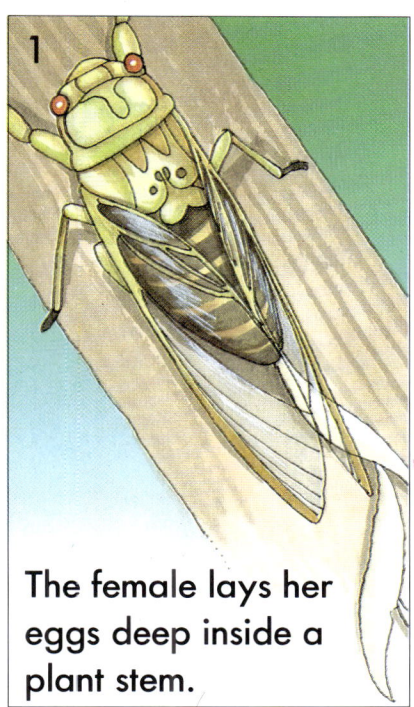

1. The female lays her eggs deep inside a plant stem.

2. The eggs lie there throughout winter and hatch in the summer.

3. A baby cicada is called a nymph. After hatching, it burrows into the ground.

4. It feeds on roots until it is fully grown. It grows wing pads.

5. It makes itself a nest under the ground. Here it lies asleep as it changes into an adult.

6. Then it climbs out of the ground and up a branch. It splits its skin and is now an adult cicada.

The Sea Urchin

This is the shell of a sea urchin. It was found on a beach.

1. The sea urchin lays its eggs in the sea.

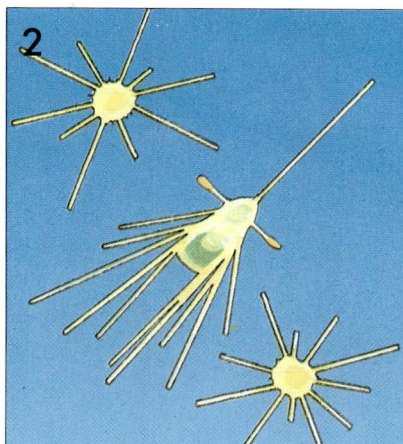

2. After hatching, the tiny sea urchin larva drifts through the water with other organisms called plankton.

3. When it changes into an adult, it grows a hard, round shell and spines.

4. Using suction feet, it glides over rocks and sand in shallow water.

5. It eats seaweed or algae, which it scrapes from the rocks with its teeth.

6. When the sea urchin dies, it rots away until only its shell is left behind.

The Monarch Butterfly

This is the chrysalis of a monarch butterfly. It was found on some milkweed.

1

The female butterfly lays her eggs on the leaves of the milkweed.

2

The caterpillar eats a hole in the eggshell and wriggles out. Then it eats the milkweed leaves.

3

The caterpillar grows bigger and bigger. As it grows, it sheds its skin.

4

When it is ready to become a chrysalis, it hangs upside-down from a twig.

5

It splits its skin for the last time and wriggles out. Now it is a green chrysalis.

6

After three weeks, the chrysalis grows darker. Finally, the skin cracks and out comes a butterfly.

The Dandelion

This is the seed head of a dandelion. It was growing under a hedge.

1

The dandelion grows a yellow flower.

2

Bees and butterflies drink nectar from the yellow flower. They spread the pollen.

3

When the flower dies, a fluffy white seed head is left.

4

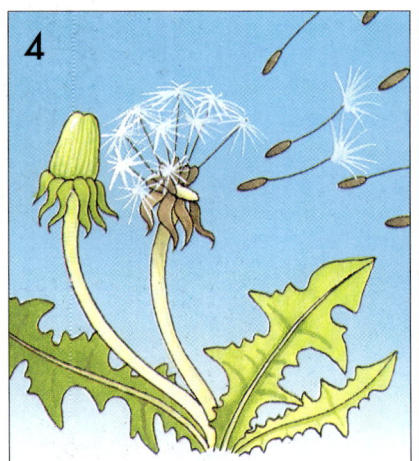

The wind blows the seed head, and the white hairs float through the air like parachutes.

5

Sometimes children help spread the seeds by blowing the dandelion heads.

6

The seeds land on the ground. New dandelion plants begin to grow.

The Thrush

This is the egg of a thrush. It was found under a tree.

1. The female thrush builds a nest. She lines the nest with mud.

2. She lays one egg a day until there are several eggs.

3. She sits on the eggs to keep them warm.

4. Twelve days later, the eggs begin to hatch.

5. The baby birds are fed insects by both their parents.

6. About two weeks after they hatch, the young thrushes leave the nest.

The Nurseryweb Spider

This is the web of a nurseryweb spider. It was found on a bush.

1. The female nurseryweb spider lays eggs in an egg sac.

2. She carries the egg sac around with her while she builds a web.

3. She weaves her nurseryweb around twigs or grass.

4. Inside the web, the baby spiders are able to hatch in safety.

5. Staying well hidden, the mother spider guards her baby spiders from enemies.

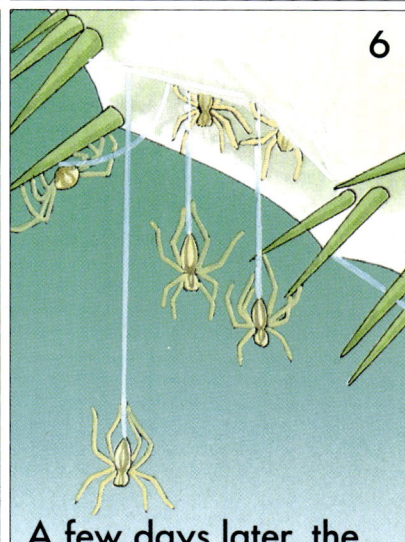

6. A few days later, the little spiders shed their skins and are ready to leave the nurseryweb.

The Pine Tree

This is a pine cone. It was found underneath a pine tree.

1

In spring, the pine tree grows male and female flowers.

2

The wind blows pollen from the male flowers to the female flowers.

3

The female flowers begin to grow into pine cones.

4

A pine cone has lots of little scales. Behind each scale there is a seed.

5

When the seed is ripe, the scale opens and the seed falls to the ground.

6

Warmth and moisture make the seed grow. A new tree has begun.

case moth
snail shell
acorn
crab shell

What can you find out about these?